S.I.M.S

First published in 1995 by
Young Library Ltd
The Old Brushworks
Pickwick Road
Corsham
Wiltshire

ISBN 1 85429 028 2

Printed in Hong Kong

Editor: Karen Foster
Designer: Ann Samuel
Artwork on pages 9,14/15, and 30/31 by Jeremy Pyke
and pages 11, 16, 17, 28, 33, 37, and 38 by Andrew Midgeley.

Picture credits: Roger Bonnett: p.9, 42, 41. Behram Kapadia: p.10,
11,13,16,19,24. Islamic Foundation: p.12,17,18,23,35(top),36.
Hutchinson Library: p.20(top), 22,25(left),27,29,32,37. Christine
Osborne: p.20(bottom), 21,25(right),26,33,34,35(bottom),39,40.

CELEBRATING

ISLAM

The customs, culture and religion of
Muslims around the world

Clive A Lawton

YOUNG LIBRARY

CONTENTS

WHAT IS ISLAM?

In the seventh century in Mecca (Makkah), a city in Saudi Arabia, lived a young man called Muhammad. Although people in Mecca worshipped many gods, Muhammad believed there was only one God, who Muslims call Allah. To serve Allah and to spread his message, Muhammad formed a new religion and preached a new way of life based on submitting to Allah's will. This new religion was called Islam, and those who follow it are called Muslims.

Muhammad's followers memorised all his teachings and wrote them down in one holy book, which is called the Koran. All Muslims believe that the Koran is the word of God, spoken to Muhammad by an angel. All aspects of Islamic life are covered in the Koran, from food to business. It also sets out five main tasks which Muslims must undertake in their lifetime. These are called the Five Pillars of Islam. Find out more about them on pages 22 and 23.

Muslims wanted everyone to share the message of the Koran. The religion spread very quickly and within 200 years Islam had penetrated into Christian Europe.

The Crusades

The Christians in Europe wanted to stop Islam spreading further and united to fight against the Muslims during the eleventh, twelfth and thirteenth centuries. The wars which were fought were called the Crusades. The Muslims were eventually driven out of Central Europe and Spain and, over the next few centuries, the Christians gained control of a large number of Muslim countries. This domination lasted right up to the twentieth century and Muslim culture was stifled.

This century Muslims began to reassert themselves, with many Muslim countries such as Iran and Iraq regaining their independence. But there is still conflict with other countries and religions. Muslims believe that Muhammad ascended into Heaven from Jerusalem in Israel, and consider it to be one of their holy cities. Therefore, when Jews expressed a wish for a Jewish state in Israel, a major political conflict between Muslims and the Jews began, which still continues today.

NOTE: Muslims throughout the world spell Mecca as Makkah.

This is the Dome of the Rock, in Jerusalem. Muslims believe that it stands on the spot from which Muhammad ascended into heaven for a night. It is one of Islam's holiest sites.

SAUDI ARABIA

PERSIAN GULF

● Mecca (Makkah)

RED SEA

This map shows you where to find Mecca in Saudi Arabia.

ISLAMIC CULTURE

Although we usually think of Islam as a religion, we should remember that religion is a set of guidelines for general living, too. You know that some binding rules were given to Muhammad by God and are written down in the Koran. Other writings, called the Hadith, contain the sayings of Muhammad, as written down by his followers after his death. The fact that all these rules are followed by Muslims all over the world makes Islam a living culture. As Islam spread throughout the world, it absorbed and influenced other cultures.

Rules for everyday life

Muhammad's teachings make several aspects of life very important to Muslims. One of these is learning. Muhammad told his followers to 'seek knowledge, even as far as China' and Muslims obeyed, learning from each community of people as they moved from country to country. Their knowledge affects much of what we know today. For example, modern mathematics started with the work of early Arab mathematicians. They even introduced the decimal point.

This is an example of Islamic art from Morocco. Find out more about patterns like these on the next page.

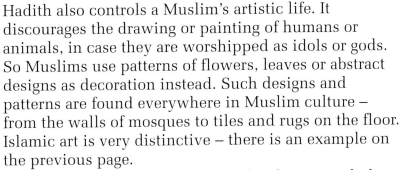

Hadith also controls a Muslim's artistic life. It discourages the drawing or painting of humans or animals, in case they are worshipped as idols or gods. So Muslims use patterns of flowers, leaves or abstract designs as decoration instead. Such designs and patterns are found everywhere in Muslim culture – from the walls of mosques to tiles and rugs on the floor. Islamic art is very distinctive – there is an example on the previous page.

Even the way Muslims greet each other is taught by Islam. The proper way is to say '**Assalaam a'alaikum**' which means '**the peace be upon you**' in Arabic. The reply is '**Wa a'alaikumassalaam**' which means '**and upon you peace**'. They are also told in which order people should be greeted: a young person should greet an elder and someone who is standing should greet someone who is sitting.

Is Muslim culture too strict?

Some Muslims want their countries to adopt a way of life which follows the laws of Islam. These people are growing in numbers and are often associated with groups called fundamentalists. Some fundamentalist groups have resorted to violence to try to put their message across.

 Find out more about . . .

The crescent and the star

The crescent and star together are the symbol of Islamic culture. No one really knows why this is, although it may be because the moon and stars are used as guides for navigation when people are travelling by night. Muslims believe that Islam guides them through life in a similar way.

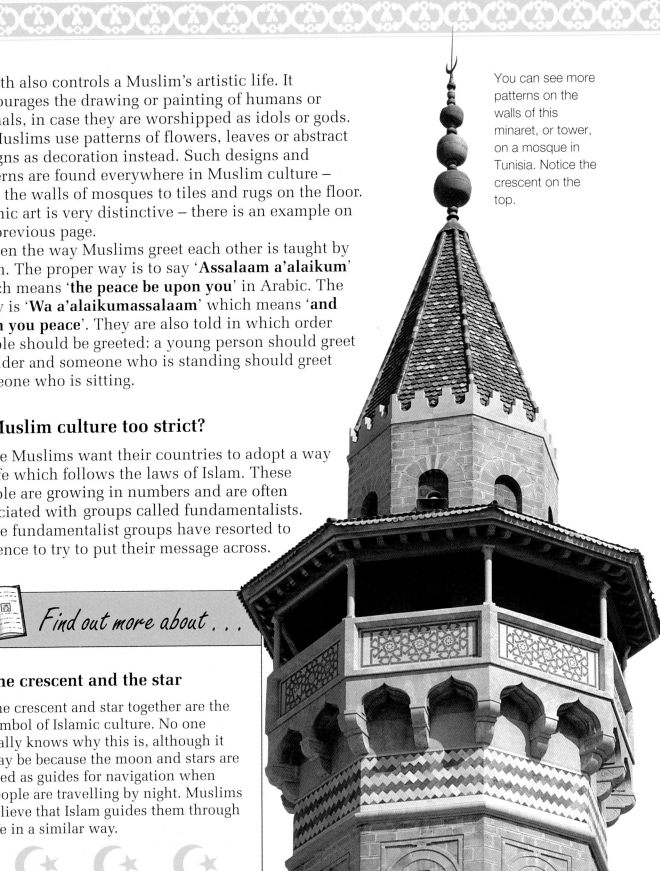

You can see more patterns on the walls of this minaret, or tower, on a mosque in Tunisia. Notice the crescent on the top.

DIFFERENT KINDS OF MUSLIMS

Muslims are Muslims wherever they are in the world. We have seen that there are large areas of the world where Islam is the main religion. But Muslims also feel a strong sense of belonging to other Muslims in all parts of the world.

This is not to say that all Muslims are alike. They have cultural differences depending on the countries in which they live, but they also have different ideas on various aspects of their history and religion.

Shi'a or Sunni?

After Muhammad died a successor had to be appointed. Some of his followers felt that the next leader should be elected by voting, which is what actually happened. These people are called Sunni, and they are the traditional followers of Islam. The majority of Muslims in the world are Sunni.

But there were others who said that the next leader should be someone from the prophet's household. They chose the nearest male relative – Ali, Muhammad's son-in-law. Muslims who accept this choice are called the Shi'ites. Shi'ites believe that there should be one leader, descended from Ali, called an imam. He has power to lead and interpret laws. The Iranian leader Ayatollah Khomeini was accepted by Shi'ites as an imam.

The Ayatollah Khomeini.

A Sunni Muslim from Kairouan in Tunisia.

Other Muslims

There are sects who believe slightly differently to the Sunnis and Shi'ites. These are often secretive, so little is known about them. Some of these sects are: the Isma'ili, whose leader is the Aga Khan; the Druze, who are a small offshoot of the Isma'ili and are found in the Lebanon and Israel; and the Sufis, who are Muslim mystics and can be either Sunni or Shi'a. They try to reach God through prayer and right behaviour. The Ahmadiya is another group who see themselves as a sect of Islam. However, most Muslims do not regard them as part of the faith.

WHERE DO MUSLIMS LIVE?

Islam is the second largest religion in the world, after Christianity, and there are estimated to be about one billion Muslims in the world. Many live in the Middle eastern and North African Arab countries, but there are large numbers in India and the East, and there is also a large and growing Muslim population in the former Soviet Union. This map shows you where Muslims live and the population for each country.

NORTH AMERICA

ATLANTIC OCEAN

SOUTH AMERICA

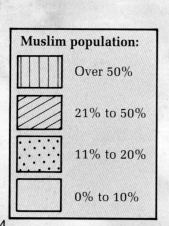

Muslim population:

⫴	Over 50%
⧄	21% to 50%
⸬	11% to 20%
☐	0% to 10%

UNITED
KINGDOM

EUROPE

AFRICA

CHINA

INDIA

PACIFIC
OCEAN

INDIAN
OCEAN

AUSTRALIA

15

THE MUSLIM LANGUAGE

Muslims believe that Arabic is special because Allah originally spoke to Muhammad in Arabic and so the original text of the Koran will always be written in Arabic. In fact, for hundreds of years Muslims did not translate it and even today all Muslims learn some Arabic so that they can read and recite parts of the holy book.

Arabic is one of the world's most widely used languages. Arab countries in modern times have become more and more important, and Arabic is now used in business and politics.

The sign on this Moroccan Coca-Cola stall is written in English and Arabic.

The Arabic alphabet

The Arabic alphabet is written on the right. There are 28 letters, with signs above and below the letters to show the vowels. Arabic is written from right to left. If this page was written in Arabic you would start reading from the top right of the page and finish at the bottom left.

Spoken Arabic, like other languages, has different dialects depending on which part of the Arab world the speaker comes from. But written Arabic is the same for everyone, except that accents are sometimes added to the text of the Koran to make it easier to read.

خ ح ج ث ت ب ا

ص ش س ز ر ذ د

ق ف غ ع ط ض

ي و ه ن م ل ك

Calligraphy

The art of decorative writing is called calligraphy. You already know that Muslims use patterns to decorate the walls of buildings, and words from the Koran written in calligraphy are often used in these patterns, especially on the walls of mosques.

The wall of this mosque is richly decorated with calligraphy.

You can...

Practise calligraphy

Use the Arabic alphabet on this page to practise calligraphy. Try to use a thick pen and smooth strokes to achieve the graceful look of this special writing. Now look back to the patterns of Islamic art on pages 10 and 11 and use some of them to decorate your calligraphy.

MUSLIM CLOTHES

This group of Muslim men are wearing a mixture of Arab clothes and western-style dress.

When people think of Muslims they think of them in long, flowing robes. Some do wear traditional clothes all the time, but many Muslims now dress in the modern clothing of the country they live in. The Koran is not very specific about clothes, but it does say that all Muslims should be modest in the way they dress.

Traditional dress

Arab clothes are long and loose. Men wear an ankle length robe called a dishdasha, or jalabiyah, which is loose trousers with a long overshirt. This way of dressing is suited to the Middle East because it is a cool and comfortable way to dress in a hot climate. On their heads they wear a white skull cap, and cover this with a red or black check scarf called a cheffiyeh. The cheffiyeh is folded in half diagonally, draped over the head and held firmly in place with a coil of black rope called an agal.

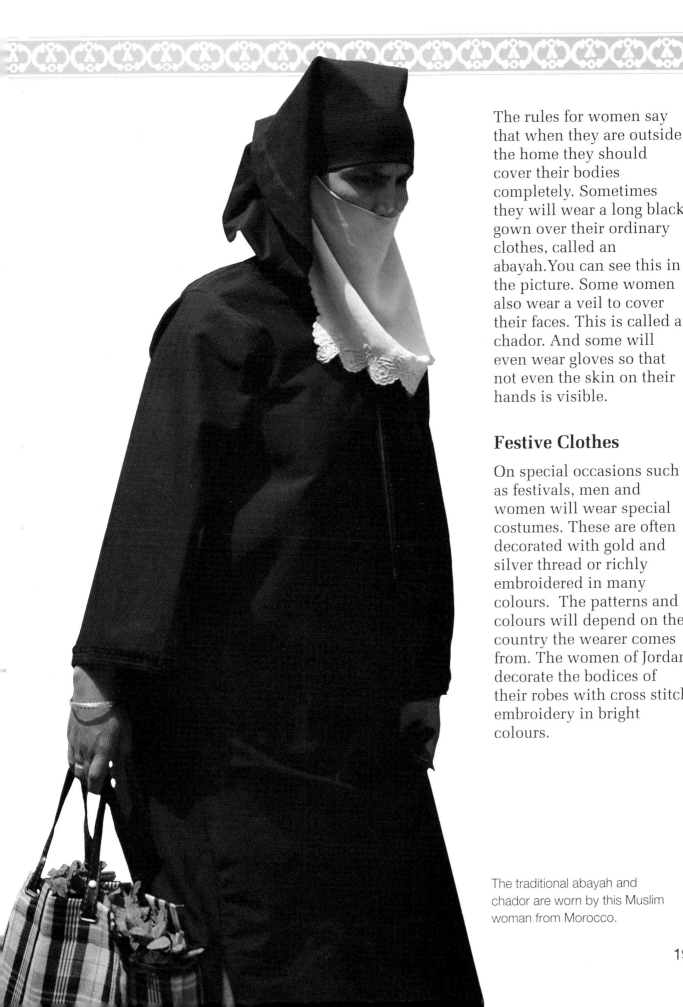

The rules for women say that when they are outside the home they should cover their bodies completely. Sometimes they will wear a long black gown over their ordinary clothes, called an abayah. You can see this in the picture. Some women also wear a veil to cover their faces. This is called a chador. And some will even wear gloves so that not even the skin on their hands is visible.

Festive Clothes

On special occasions such as festivals, men and women will wear special costumes. These are often decorated with gold and silver thread or richly embroidered in many colours. The patterns and colours will depend on the country the wearer comes from. The women of Jordan decorate the bodices of their robes with cross stitch embroidery in bright colours.

The traditional abayah and chador are worn by this Muslim woman from Morocco.

MUSLIM FOOD

Islamic culture has a great tradition of hospitality, and food plays an important part in Muslims' lives.

The Koran lays down two important rules about eating and drinking. Firstly, Muslims are forbidden to eat pork or any pig products. Any other meat they eat must be halal, which means 'permitted'. This means that the animal must be killed in the proper way, which is by cutting its throat and allowing the blood to drain away while a blessing is said over it. To make sure that they are eating halal meat, Muslims buy their meat from special Halal butchers.

Secondly, Muslims are not allowed to drink alcohol, and in many Muslim countries it is against the law to do so. Instead they often drink thick, sweet coffee or tea flavoured with mint or lemon. Coffee drinking is a national pastime in many Muslim countries and there are special coffee houses where people meet.

You may have already tried Turkish Delight or pastries like baklava, which is made from honey and nuts. Both of these sweets come from Islamic countries. Fruits such as apricots are added to Muslim meat dishes - chicken and apricots is a Moroccan delicacy.

A group of Muslims drinking coffee.

A traditional sweet from Jordan called knaffeh.

Find out more about...

Muslim meals

Muslims always wash their hands before they sit down to eat a meal and a prayer is said before the meal begins. Families will wait until the oldest person starts to eat before they do, as a sign of respect. In some Muslim countries families who have prepared a meal for a guest will wait until the guest has completely finished eating before they start to eat.

A Muslim family in England say a prayer before they begin their meal.

THE KORAN

You know that the Muslim holy book, the Koran, gives guidelines for a proper Islamic life. The word Koran means 'recitation' in Arabic. This is because every Muslim has a duty to read and recite the Koran, so that they know what God wants them to do. Muslims also turn to the Koran to help them in times of crisis or uncertainty. They even learn parts of it by heart. Anyone who learns the whole of the Koran by heart is given the honorary title of Hafiz.

The Koran is divided into 114 chapters which are called surahs. Some surahs are very short, with only three or four sentences. Others are very long. The longest is Surah 2 which has 286 verses. If you want to look something up in the Koran and you are told it is in 114:4, that means you must look at the 114th surah and at the fourth verse in that surah.

These boys from London obey the rule in the Koran which says Muslims must wash before they pray.

The Five Pillars

Apart from the rules for general living, Muhammad gave five rules for life, called the Five Pillars of Islam. The first pillar is the most important. It is the declaration of faith in Allah. For someone to become a Muslim they have to say the declaration, called the Shahadah and in Arabic it is: '**La ilaha illa Allah, Muhammadan**

This decorated copy of the Koran rests on its own wooden stand.

Rasulu Allah'. It means 'There is no God but Allah and Muhammad is his prophet'.

The second pillar is prayer. Muslims must pray five times a day, at dawn, noon, mid-afternoon, sunset and night. They sometimes need to interrupt their other activities to do this, which reminds them of their submission to God. Before they can pray they must wash their face and hands and feet. According to the Koran Muslims must do this unless they are ill, travelling or fighting in battle.

The third pillar is a kind of welfare tax. Muslims are expected to give about 2.5% of their annual savings to their relatives, orphans, the needy, travellers and to those who ask. This is called zakat. Other charity is also very important to Muslims and they must always be ready to give it.

The fourth and fifth pillars are fasting and pilgrimage which we will learn about later.

 Find out more about...

Owning a copy of the Koran

Muslims keep their own copies of the Koran very carefully. Usually the book is wrapped in cloth so that it does not get dirty. When the Koran is taken out to be read, it is placed on a low wooden stand so that it does not touch the floor. These stands are carved into beautiful patterns and they fold up so that they are easily carried.

A PLACE TO PRAY

This huge mosque in Tunisia has two minarets and a large golden dome.

Muslims say their daily prayers wherever they are — at home, at work, or in a mosque. In small communities a mosque might be in a house or a hall, but in large towns and cities there is often a purpose built mosque. You can see they are large and beautiful, but also very simple in design.

The first things you will notice about a traditional mosque are the large dome and the tower. The dome sits above the main prayer hall and helps to echo the prayers around the mosque. The tower is outside the mosque and is called a minaret. From the top of the minaret a mosque official called a muezzin calls the Muslims to prayer. Nowadays an amplifier is used.

Before entering the mosque, Muslims must take off their shoes and wash their hands, face and feet. There will be a place for washing at the entrance. It used to be a fountain, but now there is a tiled room with taps.

Inside the mosque

There may be many rooms inside the mosque but the main prayer room is a large space where there is no furniture. Muslims do not sit on seats when they pray but sit or kneel on mats on the floor. They do not need tables for their prayer books, either, because they know all their prayers off by heart. Muslims use several ritual prayer movements: standing, kneeling and touching their heads to the floor.

The whole congregation faces the direction of Mecca, which is the holy place we heard about on page 8. It is shown by a small alcove called a mihrab. There is also a platform called a minbar, where the leader of the service, or Imam, stands to give his Friday sermon.

Women do not pray with men. They pray in a section separated from the men, where they can hear the prayers but are not seen. Often a screen blocks them off from the main hall.

Muslim men at prayer at a mosque in London.

You can...

Listen to the muezzin

The muezzin's call is a truly amazing sound, and one which is hard to describe. Why don't you try to hear it for yourself? Find out if you have a local mosque and try to visit it at one of the Islamic prayer times (look back to page 23 to see when these are). You should be able to hear the muezzin from outside the mosque. If this is impossible, perhaps you can find a recording of a muezzin in your local library.

The muezzin calls.

TRADITIONS

The Muslim culture has many ceremonies which are used to celebrate special happenings in their lives.

The birth of a child

A child born to a Muslim family is considered to be a Muslim from the moment it is born. The first words that a baby hears are the declaration of faith or the first Pillar of Islam as described on page 20. When the baby is seven days old it receives its name in a ceremony called Aqiqa. The name given is usually a name with special significance – the name of a relative the parents wish to honour, or one of Muhammad's names, or one of the 99 names of Allah. Part of the ceremony is shaving the baby's hair. The hair is weighed and its weight in silver is given to the poor. Then an animal is sacrificed and the meat is shared between the family and the poor. These ceremonies give thanks for the birth.

Marriage

Muslim society is founded on the family, so stable marriages are very important. A Muslim man is allowed to have up to four wives. However, the Koran tells him that each of the wives must be treated equally. This is very difficult to do, so in practice men will often have only one wife.

Muslim marriages are often 'arranged' by older relatives. But as the Koran says that no man or woman must marry against their will, people do have some choice. In the marriage ceremony the bride and bridegroom sign a contract in front of two Muslim witnesses. Friends and relatives often give the couple presents of money, as in this picture.

A Muslim couple celebrate their wedding in Egypt.

You can...

Estimate the worth of a baby's hair

Can you think how much money a new born baby's hair would be worth if you were following the Muslim custom? Of course, it would vary quite a lot because some babies have more hair than others. But estimate that a baby's hair weighs two ounces, then look in today's paper to find out the price of silver per ounce. Now work it out!

After death

As Muslim people are dying they try to say or hear the declaration of faith for the last time. After death the body is wrapped in three white sheets, and in Muslim countries it is buried without a coffin. This is because Muslims prefer to be buried in direct contact with the earth, with their head pointing to Mecca. The grave has no headstone. Mourning goes on for three days, when friends and relatives visit the family. Muslims firmly believe in life after death, so death to them is just a staging post as they pass from one life to the next.

A funeral procession in the Sudan. A sheet is draped over the body as it is carried to the grave.

JUMA

The Muslims have a special day every week which is Friday, called Juma in Arabic. Muslims are encouraged to visit the mosque to say noon prayers on this day, and to listen to the weekly sermon given by the Imam.

Unlike Shabbat for Jews and Sunday for Christians, Juma is not a day when work or business are forbidden. Although Muslims do all try and attend the mosque, and children often leave school early so that they can accompany their parents to pray, it is just as important to meet up with friends and relatives to talk and share meals at home.

In the evening, children may attend the mosque to meet their friends and learn about Islam from the Imam. They take lessons in Arabic so that they can read the Koran and learn how to live a proper Islamic life.

All over the world, children spend time reading the Koran on Fridays. This boy is from Oman, in the Persian Gulf.

You can...

Make pita biscuits

In India, pita biscuits are often served with the evening meal on Juma. Here's how to make them.

1 Mix 100g rice flour with 100g sugar and a pinch of salt.

2 Beat 2 eggs together, then gently add them to the mixture and stir until you have a thick dough.

3 Roll out the dough to 1/2 cm thick.

4 Cut into small squares, then roll each one into a ball and flatten it slightly between your hands.

5 Fry the biscuits in vegetable oil, turning them until they are golden-brown and puffy.
ASK AN ADULT TO HELP YOU WITH THE FRYING.

Month
Zulkadah (30 days)

Month
Zulhijjah (29 days)
Festival
The Hajj (Pilgrimage to Mecca)
Eid ul Adha
(Festival of sacrifice)

Month
Shawwal (29 days)

Festival
Eid ul Fitr (end of Ramadan)

THE MUSLIM CALENDAR

The solar year is 365 days long, which is the time it takes for the earth to orbit the sun. In the Muslim year there are only 354 days. This is the time it takes for the moon to go around the earth twelve times. Imagine that Muslim New Year is on 1st January this year. Next year it will

Month
Ramadan (30 days)

Festival
Ramadan (Month of Fasting)
Lailat ul Qadr (Night of Power)
Celebrates the night when
Muhammad received
God's message.

Month
Sha'baan (29 days)

Festival
Lailat ul Bara'at
(Night of Forgiveness).
Prayers are said to ask
forgiveness for wrong
doing.

Month
Rajab (30 days)

Festival
Lailat ul Mi'raj (Night of Ascent)
Celebrates Muhammad's
ascent into heaven.

Month
Muharram (30 days long)

Festival
Muharram (New Year)

Month
Safar (29 days)

Month
Rabi 'al-Awwal (30 days)

Festival
Milad-an-Nabi
(Muhammad's birthday)

Month
Rabi 'al-Akhir (29 days)

be on December 19th, and it will only be the 1st of January again in 32.5 years time! You can see that it doesn't take long before a winter festival becomes a summer one. The Arabic names of the Islamic months are given here, together with the festivals which occur during each one.

Let's say that Muharram, the first month of the Muslim year, falls in January this year. Follow the months round to Zulhijjah. In which Muslim month would your birthday fall?

Month
Jumada' al-Akhirah (29 days)

Month
Jumada' al-Ula (30 days)

RAMADAN

The ninth month of the Islamic year is called Ramadan. It is the most holy month for Muslims, because the angel first spoke to Muhammad in this month. During Ramadan, Muslims do not eat or drink during daylight hours. Why do they do it?

They face this challenge because they want to show that they are prepared to submit to the will of Allah. They learn what it is like to be hungry and poor and they remember to be generous and kind to the needy, as the Koran tells them to be.

Because the solar date of Muslim festivals changes every year, Ramadan can fall in the summer or the winter. In a northern country like Britain, the hours of daylight are few in the winter so fasting from sunrise to sunset might not be so bad. Perhaps it might just mean skipping lunch. But in the summer Ramadan is a real challenge when it can be daylight for up to 18 hours!

Not all Muslims need to keep strictly to the rules. Pregnant women, old and sick people, those travelling and young children would find it difficult or dangerous and are therefore not required to fast. Families who fast together in Ramadan feel closer and therefore everyone tries to go without food for some of the time.

Muslims at a mosque in England during Ramadan. The declaration of faith in English and Arabic is on the wall of the mosque.

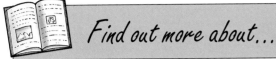

Find out more about...

Meals during Ramadan

Of course, Muslims have to eat at some time during Ramadan. Before dawn they eat a meal called suhur. Then, after sunset they break their fast by eating something small like a piece of fruit and sipping some water. Then they pray. The evening meal is called iftar. You can imagine how hungry they are by this time.

Olives and dates are often eaten to break the Ramadan fast each evening.

A family from Bahrain in the Persian Gulf eat their meal before dawn during Ramadan.

EID UL FITR

Everyone is eagerly awaiting the end of Ramadan. They have been fasting for a month and are looking forward to the end of it. The festival of fast-breaking, Eid ul Fitr, is held on the first day of the month after Ramadan.

Muslim months begin at the very moment the new moon appears. So as soon as the new moon has been sighted, Muslims get ready for the festival that follows.

The festival begins with prayers. Everyone dresses in their best clothes to visit the mosque. Children may stay away from school because it is an important time to be

In some Muslim countries, even the buildings are decorated for Eid ul Fitr. Coloured lights have been hung on this building in Abu Dhabi, a city in the United Arab Emirates.

Design a card for Eid

Muslims who are separated from their families traditionally send cards to celebrate Eid. The design often includes the greeting **'Eid Mubarak'** which means 'Happy Festival' in Arabic. Try designing your own card for Eid, using the greeting as part of your design. Remember that there are examples of Islamic art on pages 10 and 11 if you want to use them.

This picture shows you a selection of Eid cards.

together with their family and community. After visiting the mosque there is a family meal. Children are given presents of sweets or new clothes. In countries like Saudi Arabia there is singing and dancing and camel racing.

Ramadan gives people sympathy and understanding for the poor, so at this festival Muslims give extra money. This charity is called sadaqah, and is as well as the regular tax, or zakat, which you read about on page 23.

Many mosques have special boxes for sadaqah and zakat money.

HAJJ

Every Muslim wants to go on a pilgrimage to Mecca, their holy city. This pilgrimage is called the Hajj, and most Muslims try to go on the Hajj at least once in their lives. It happens in the twelfth month of each Islamic year, and about two million Muslims arrive in Mecca at the same time.

On arrival, each pilgrim washes and changes into a simple white gown, an ihram. This is a type of uniform which makes them all equal, so they can forget their wealth or nationality and stand as one before God.

The ceremonies take five days. When pilgrims arrive in Mecca, they enter the courtyard of the Great Mosque to visit the huge stone building which is called the Kabah. Muslims believe that the Kabah was built by the prophet Abraham and his son as a place to worship God. A vast crowd of Muslims circles the Kabah seven times. This custom is

During Hajj, the courtyard of the Great Mosque is filled with pilgrims circling the Kabah.

This family of pilgrims from Malaysia are all dressed in the simple white gown called an ihram.

called the tawaf. As they pass the black stone on the corner of the Kabah, each pilgrim raises his hand in salute.

Then the pilgrims visit a well called Zamzam, which is near the Kabah. When Hagar, Abraham's wife, was in the desert with their son and had no water, God gave her a miraculous spring. This water is drunk by the pilgrims and they also take some home to their families.

The pilgrims must then travel nine miles from Mecca to the Plain of Mina, where Muhammad delivered his final sermon. They spend three days in prayer and sleep out in the open. They also go to the Valley of Mina where Abraham was tempted by the devil. Then they sacrifice an animal to commemorate Abraham's sacrifice, which you can read about over the page. Finally, they return to the Kabah to perform tawaf one last time, before returning home. Everyone who has been on the Hajj is given the title of Hajji, and all their friends congratulate them on their pilgrimage.

Find out more about . . .

The valley of Mina

When the devil appeared to Abraham in the valley of Mina, he tried to persuade Abraham not to obey God's wishes. He tempted Abraham three times, and three times Abraham threw stones at Satan to drive him away. Pilgrims today throw pebbles at stone pillars to remind them of Abraham's strength of will.

EID UL ADHA

At the time of the Hajj there is a joyful celebration called Eid ul Adha which is celebrated all over the world wherever there are Muslims, so that they all feel part of the Hajj. In Arab countries, there are parties in the streets, and everywhere Muslims give each other presents.

The story of Abraham

The festival is held to remember the story of Abraham. Allah wanted to test Abraham so he told him to kill his own son. Abraham had such trust in Allah that he immediately set off to Mina to do so, even though he loved his son very much. On his way, Abraham was tempted by the devil, who wanted him to disobey Allah – you heard about this on the previous page. When Abraham proved that he was even prepared to give up his son for Allah, Allah told him to sacrifice a goat instead.

Muslims remember this at Eid ul Adha by killing an animal, as an offering to God. In Muslim countries they buy a specially fattened sheep, goat or cow from the market as a sacrifice.

The animal is killed in the same way that Muslims kill animals for food, although in some countries the body is covered with a special cloth and decorations are placed on the head. But after the animal has been killed, the meat is divided into three parts. One part is given to the poor, the second to friends and relatives and the last part is eaten by the family. While they are eating the meat, Muslims think about the story of Abraham, and enjoy being part of the Muslim community all over the world.

Brightly-coloured decorations like this shield are made from tinsel to decorate animals for Eid ul Adha. Presents and sweets are given to celebrate the festival.

These fattened goats have been decorated ready for the Eid ul Adha festival in Pakistan.

ISLAM ALL AROUND

Now that you know something about Islam, its culture and its followers, there are many ways in which you can start to be more aware of Muslims and their faith in the world around you.

Think about other people

Firstly, think about Muslim people themselves. You may already have a Muslim friend, who can tell you what it is really like to follow Islam. Or you can find other books to read about Islam. Think about how Muslims fit in prayer times with their work routine – perhaps they have to give up the free time during breaks to visit the mosque. Don't forget that there might well be Muslims in the place where you live, each enjoying being part of the rich culture of Islam.

Muslims greet each other after prayers at a London mosque.

You can even take more of an interest in Muslim food! Look on the shelves of your local supermarket to see which foods have labels written in Arabic. You might be able to try out recipes from a Muslim country if you find the right cookbook.

Be aware of current events

When you listen to the news, or read a newspaper, you will probably come across events connected with Islam and its people. These events are not always happy ones – turn back to page 11 to remind yourself about Islamic fundamentalists. These groups are often in the news because of their extreme political views. But they are a minority, so notice other events, too – perhaps pictures of the huge number of pilgrims visiting Mecca this year or a new mosque being built in your town.

The influence of Islamic architecture is a common sight in countries like Tunisia. In this picture, you can see a city gate with a mosque in the background.

Look around you

When you are in a town or city, try to find out whether there is a local mosque. If you are on holiday, make an effort to visit a mosque so that you can compare it to mosques you have seen at home. Keep an eye out for the influence of Islamic art and architecture in buildings around you – a curved archway like the one in this picture is a good example, and something you may see if you travel abroad.

QUIZ

Here are some puzzles and questions to test your knowledge of Islam. All the solutions can be found somewhere in this book. When you've finished, look at the answers at the bottom of the page. Make sure you do not mark the book.

1 What is the symbol of Islamic culture?

2 Which food and drinks are forbidden to Muslims?

3 Name the alcove found in the wall of each mosque which faces Mecca.

4 Name the city shown on this map detail.

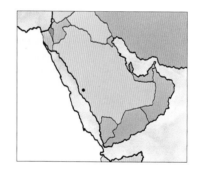

5 What is the name given to meat that has been prepared according to Islamic law?

6 Why do pilgrims throw pebbles at stone pillars in the valley of Mina?

7 Can you recognise this place from the detail of this photograph?

8 What is the name of the special charity given to the poor for Eid ul Fitr?

9 How many letters are there in the Arabic alphabet?

10 What is the name given to the wars fought between Christians and Muslims over 800 years ago?

11 Unscramble these letters to find the name of a famous Shi'ite Muslim: I H A Y O E N A K A H T L O L M I.

12 During which month of the Islamic year does Ramadan fall?

13 Fill in the empty spaces to find the name of the tower found on each mosque: M – – A – E – .

14 What must Muslims do before they enter a mosque to pray?

15 What does the word 'Koran' mean in Arabic?

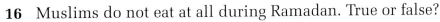

16 Muslims do not eat at all during Ramadan. True or false?

17 What are the Five Pillars of Islam?

18 What happens to the meat of animals sacrificed for Eid ul Adha?

19 Does Ramadan fall in Summer or Winter?

20 Some words connected with Islam have all been hidden in this word box. They might be printed across, upwards or downwards, or diagonally but always in a straight line. You can use letters more than once. Can you find these 10 words:

ARABIC,

EID,

HAJJ,

HALAL,

ISLAM,

JUMA,

KORAN,

MECCA,

MOSQUE

MUSLIM?

L	B	I	F	H	J	U	M	A	H
M	O	S	Q	U	E	T	C	S	A
U	R	L	Y	D	C	I	I	G	L
S	C	A	L	I	K	H	B	R	A
L	T	M	U	E	K	O	A	O	L
I	N	E	P	E	R	B	R	B	V
M	E	C	C	A	G	D	A	A	S
B	Q	R	A	H	A	J	J	E	N

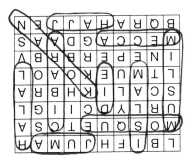

Glossary

abayah
A long black gown worn by Muslim women.

agal
A coil of black rope used to keep an Arab man's headscarf in place.

Allah
The Islamic name for God.

Aqiqa
The naming ceremony for Muslim babies.

Arabic
The official language of Arab countries, and a special language for Muslims because the original text of the Koran was given to Muhammad in Arabic.

chador
The veil worn by Muslim women.

cheffiyeh
The red or black checked headscarf worn by Muslim men.

dishdasha
An ankle-length robe worn by Muslim men.

Eid ul Adha
The festival of sacrifice which celebrates the end of the Hajj.

Eid ul Fitr
The festival of fast-breaking which marks the end of Ramadan.

Five pillars of Islam
The five main tasks which each Muslim should undertake. They are: the declaration of faith, prayer, charity, fasting and pilgrimage.

Hadith
The sayings of the prophet Muhammad.

Hafiz
The honorary title given to anyone who learns the whole of the Koran by heart.

Hajj
The name given to the Muslim pilgrimage to Mecca.

halal
Meat which has been prepared according to Islamic law is halal.

iftar
The evening meal during Ramadan.

ihram
The white gown which each pilgrim wears during Hajj.

Koran
The Muslim holy book.

Makkah
The official Muslim spelling of Mecca.

Mecca (Makkah)
Muhammad's birthplace, a city in Saudi Arabia.

mihrab
The alcove in the wall of each mosque which faces Mecca.

minaret
The tower above each mosque from which Muslims are called to prayer.

mosque
A building used for Muslim prayer.

muezzin
The official who calls Muslims to prayer.

Ramadan
The month of fasting.

religion
An organised system of beliefs and practices, usually centred on a God, or gods.

sacrifice
The killing of an animal as an offering to God.

sadaqah
The charity given at festivals like Ramadan.

Shahadah
The Arabic name for the Muslim declaration of faith.

suhur
The meal taken before dawn during Ramadan.

tawaf
The name given to the ritual circling of the Kabah during the Hajj.

zakat
The Arabic word for a welfare tax.

44

Index